JEREMY SHARES HIS LOVE FROM ABOVE

JEREMY SHARES HIS LOVE FROM ABOVE

A guide to living joyously on Earth following the passing of a loved one and always!

JEREMY LOGUE
RHONDA CROCKETT LOGUE
& ANTONIETTE IBUSAG

NEXT CENTURY
PUBLISHING

Jeremy Shares His Love From Above

Published by Next Century Publishing
Austin, Texas
www.NextCenturyPublishing.com

Initial Cover Design and Editing Performed By Carley Bennecke

ISBN: 978-1-64339-931-7

Printed in the United States of America

Acknowledgements

I am excited and grateful to share this book with you and hope that it will fill you with knowledge, joy, and peace! I, Jeremy, would like to share information that will assist you in living peacefully on Earth. But first, I would like to thank my mom for always listening to me and believing in me. I love her so much. I could not bring this information to you without her. She lovingly and faithfully listened to me as I provided the information for this book.

I also want to thank my family and friends for my wonderful Earth experience and for always loving me. My dad is the best father, and he always inspired me to be the greatest person I could be. My brothers, Michael and Nicholas, I love them so much. I enjoyed all the adventures we shared on Earth and those we continue to share. My sisters, Megan and Rachel, I am still with you, loving you, and kicking your butts in soccer. Ha! I had the best extended Earth family that anyone could ask for. They were always loving, caring, and accepting of me. My Earth friends are loyal and true, and we still share good times. My Earth girlfriend, Antoniette, I thank you for loving me and teaching me to love no matter what. Thank you, Antoniette, for hearing me and participating in the creation of this book and for adding your astonishing love and light. Shine bright, Babe, and I look forward to our next book together, coming soon.

This book is structured with information to help you now, as you might presently be struggling in your journey of grieving for a loved one who has passed from this lifetime. This information is provided to assist you in living with peace and joy for the rest of your Earth life.

I love you!

Jeremy

Jeremy Shares His Love From Above
is an enlightening book of love, wisdom, and guidance.
It will inspire those who have loved ones who
have passed from this lifetime and guide those who wish to
know how to live a peaceful life on Earth.

Jeremy beautifully channels his information
to his mother and to the love of his life, his Earth
girlfriend, to bring this book to you!

Beware, it could possibly change your life!

Reviews

"*Jeremy Shares His Love From Above is an extraordinary book. It has a powerful message and offers much enlightenment. Jeremy's words bring a deep sense of peace, happiness, and understanding. I love everything I learned about life, spirit, relationships, and myself. Thank you, Jeremy!*"
-Linda Rash

"*The enlightening information presented in this book brings much joy to the reader. It quickly shifts one's mood to love and happiness!*"
-Melinda Tobacco

"*Jeremy's book has given me a new perspective on life. I now love every obstacle presented to me, good or bad. I appreciate every day and have learned to turn everything negative into a positive. Thank you, Jeremy! I am grateful for your wonderful words of wisdom!*"
-Michelle Espitia

"I truly enjoyed reading Jeremy Shares His Love From Above. It is very inspiring! I enjoyed reading about Jeremy's caring heart and seeing his big, beautiful smile!"
-Dana Hockett

"I would like to thank Rhonda and Jeremy for sharing this uplifting and inspiring book that is filled with love. I cried as I began reading, but then I felt Jeremy's love and happiness. This book came to me at the perfect time when I was feeling lost from experiencing the passing of several close family members. I realized while reading Jeremy's book that I had stopped listening to my own divine guidance. I understand now that my life lessons are to learn from my experiences. I realize how important it is to listen to my Soul's messages. Now I feel so much more gladness, peace, and inspiration that I haven't felt in a long time!"
-Lorraine Arensdorff

Contents

JEREMY SHARES
HIS LOVE
FROM ABOVE

Foreword

For those who knew Jeremy during his lifetime, they would tell you that Jeremy was one to speak his mind. He confronted issues head-on. He would speak up when something said was untrue. He would try to prove his point, and we would listen and think, *What is he talking about?* but still say, "Okay, Jeremy." Jeremy knew things, and we couldn't figure out how he knew them. Jeremy did things, and we couldn't figure out how he did them. Jeremy wrote inspiring words of wisdom that were far beyond his years.

Little did we know that much of his wisdom he shared during his lifetime was just above our awareness and understanding at that time.

The information Jeremy presents in this book may be above many awarenesses as well, but if you allow his information to settle, you will know from the depths of your Heart and Soul that it is Truth!

Jeremy wishes only the best for all of us as we embark upon our Journeys, that which we call life.

CHAPTER 1

You Never Leave Your Loved Ones

Hi, my name is Jeremy Eugene Logue. I passed from my Earth Life the day after Father's Day on June 20, 2016. It was the day of a Summer Solstice and the night of a Strawberry Moon. I was in a car accident and I transitioned quickly into my Spirit form, leaving my physical body behind. But, I did not leave! Your loved ones who have transitioned want you to know that they are fine and well and they are always with you. Like Always!

Once we transform into Spirit form, we can be many places. I can be with Aunt Sue and Cousin Kathy, who are in different areas, at the same time. This is so cool! We hear your every thought and word and we see your Spirit form. We are always communicating with your Spirit and sharing our love and guidance with you. What we want more than anything is for our loved ones to feel us and to hear us. Seeing us is great too. You may see us how you remember us in our physical form or as a ball of light energy. Remember, we no longer have our physical bodies. But we can project an image that appears like our physical bodies so you can recognize us. We are always with you. Call our name or think of us and: *boom*. We are there with you. Many people do not see or hear us because they think that they cannot when, in fact, animals and young children converse with us all the time. Young children and animals do not yet have the blocks that adult humans have developed. My mom will tell you that I had an "imaginary friend," as many would call it, when I was younger named George, who taught me to do spit wads.

My mom never told me to not trust what I heard and saw. Rather, she said, "Who else would have taught him to do that?" She believed me when we passed a traffic accident and I said, "The lady is floating above the car." That person had passed in the car accident.

Unfortunately, when children share what they see and hear and no one else can see or hear it, many adults tell them that it's pretend or that it's all in their heads.

The adults were most likely told the same thing when they were young, so you can't blame them. However, the children then stop believing what they see and hear, which is usually their Divine Guidance. It gets worse. Kids then begin to disbelieve many things that they know to be true. They begin to lose sight of who they are because they are now believing what they are told to believe.

They lose sight of their true essence, which is unconditional love and trusting in their Divine Source (what many would know as God, Buddha, etc.). Our Divine Source has all the guidance and answers for us to live peacefully and joyfully on Earth and can teach us how to maintain our true selves of unconditional love!

CHAPTER 2

You Are Still Pure Love Even When You Feel That You Are Not

One of my life lessons was to share unconditional love. I saw my friends for who they truly were even when they could not see it. One of my best Earth friends had some problems, as we all do. He struggled with losses and he did not always handle his pain well. I loved him just how he was, and when my parents expressed concern for me hanging around him, I would tell my parents, "You don't know him like I do. He is a good person." I saw him for who he was, which was pure, unconditional love.

Another reason we lose sight of who we genuinely are is because emotions, beliefs, and traumas from our Earth experiences can become stuck to us, resulting in our true selves getting buried deep inside us. We forget who we are. We forget about our connection to everyone, everything, and even to our Divine Source.

It's like this. We are born with absolute pure love at birth. However, our experiences with parents, society, school, work, friends, and Earth life can contribute to blocking our awareness of our true essence, our true being, our Spirit. We adopt the beliefs of others that are foreign to our Souls. For example, a doctor may wish for their child to also become a doctor. The child might feel pressure to become a doctor even though that is not their true passion. For parents, it is important to be aware of this so as to not interfere with their child's greatness and natural gifts. For it is only when they remain pure love or return to pure love do they see and recognize their child's true gifts and potential. Parents can help by allowing their child to be who they are or not discouraging and steering their child away from their true path.

My mom, who loved me so much, did not want me to enter into the Air Force because she thought she knew better than me. She did it out of love and protection for her child, but I continued my Divine Path of efforts with the Air Force and hid it from my mom so she would not discourage me. I loved practicing for the Air

Force and flying. That was my passion. I did not let my mom's thoughts get in the way of it. However, it did put a distance between us because I felt deceitful.

That being said, my point is that many kids fall into the trap of not following their true passion. Even worse is not remaining in their pure love essence due to influences. These influences can turn into self doubt, which can then formulate negative beliefs, changing who you are and how you behave until your pure love essence gets put on the back burner. Then it is difficult to retrieve again sometimes. You begin living your life, not from your joy, but from everyone else's expectations for you until you don't even remember who you are, which is pure love. You are still pure love even when you do not feel it. But the good news is, you can remember who you are. You can remember!

CHAPTER 3

You Can Remember

Now you may have obtained a life far from your true passion instead of living a life in line with your true passion. No worries. Many people on Earth do this. They get lost. I did to an extent, but I continued to fight it. Some teachers and even my parents thought I was rude when I voiced my thoughts and opinions about a lame rule I did not want to comply with. The rule just wasn't for me, or good for me. Others think they know what is best for us. The truth is, we know what is best for us.

Anyhow, some people simply comply with things that do not resonate with their Souls. Examples are health care, taxes, religion, laws, regulations. You lose control from exhaustion and allow others to take over and run your life. You forget who you truly are, and you're just being someone and doing something you are not. Then your true passion goes out the window. What you came here in this lifetime to do becomes hidden, even buried. You keep doing the same thing, believing the same beliefs, and functioning at a state that does not feel good to the Soul.

We are all unique. We all have our own special talents and passions that we choose to live. We also have our own unique struggles and pain episodes that we create to direct us back to our Soul's purpose. This was all designed by you in your Soul Contract. I will discuss more on Soul Contracts later in Chapter 9. The most important thing to know when returning to your purest state, which is pure unconditional love, is: "That is exactly what you are right now" except that you may not see it or remember it because the negative energy is trapped in you. All the untrue beliefs you adopted from others. All the difficult situations or traumas that occurred. You choose to hold onto the depression, grief, or shame from them, instead of trusting your Divine Source and moving through the storm.

Release the trapped energy stuck in you, and then you will remember who you really are, a Divine Being of only unconditional love, nothing else.

I am sure you are asking, "But how do I release the trapped energy?" First you must be willing to let it go! People get so accustomed to their trapped energy and want to hold onto the negativity even when this energy is causing illness, depression, and all sorts of problems. You may wonder, *Why do they hold onto the trapped energy?* It's because it is familiar to them since they have had it for so long. It feels safe. The mind tries to protect us and keep us safe, but the mind is really keeping us stuck by holding onto energy that's not in our best interest. When you try to release negative energy, the mind is replying, "Don't do it," "You'll get hurt," and "It's not safe." But your Soul is exclaiming, "Free yourself," "You deserve to be free," and "Remember, you are only love."

To be willing to "let go" of trapped negative energy is a choice. A good question to ask yourself is, "Do I want Peace or do I want Bondage?" It's your choice. Your Soul will provide experiences and life lessons to push you towards Peace. The more you resist, the more experiences and life lessons come your way, encouraging you to fall into alignment with your Soul Path. When you choose not to resist, you ride the tide, allowing all to flow, even what is unpleasant. Then the unpleasantness moves through more quickly and you find the peace, guidance, and serenity you are desiring.

You can get to a point in your life where you are living from your Higher Self (aware and enlightened self) guided by your Divine Source and you feel the joy in all situations even when the situations may not seem so joyful. This is a sweet way to live, and it is the way your Soul and your Divine Source wants you to live. There is always a gift and an enlightenment in every situation. So, remember who you are and you will move easily through life situations and live in joy. You deserve it!

CHAPTER 4

Did You Know . . .

Did you know you were not designed to go through life on your own? Did you know that your Heavenly loved ones, Spirits, Guides, Angels, and even Source or God Energy are always with you, guiding your every step? Did you know they love you so much that they are holding you even when you choose a difficult path? Did you know they experience emotions, including sadness when you struggle, but they know that you are learning a life lesson you chose to learn? Did you know they are supporting and guiding every step of your journey?

Unfortunately, as stated previously in this book, many of us lose sight of our Divine connection in childhood and go through life feeling disconnected and not understanding why.

We feel lost from our true Source, our home, our everything. It is generally through trauma and hardship that the feelings of loss intensify, and then the search for understanding and truth begins. The search is for your complete self, which includes your Divine connection. You see, we are all one. We are all connected, and our Divine support never leaves us. However, it can become buried. Many will not trust their Divine guidance. They will not trust what they hear, feel, know, and see. They will go through life feeling alone. This is *resistance*. Resistance to what your Soul and Spirit knows to be true. But as you are learning, knowledge and enlightenment is Power. Power is what you seek. Power to regain true Divine connection, which will remind you that all is well, and to allow energy, good or what you might consider bad, to flow. Not to get stuck and trapped in you. Trapped energy causes ailments, sadness, depression, and more. Who would want that?

Therefore, empower yourselves with the truth. Feel the truth deeply as your Soul and Spirit raves and cheers you on.

Divine helpers are cheering you on too!

CHAPTER 5

Can You Hear Me?

Listen. Listen to the birds sing. Listen to the dishes bang. If you lived in my house, you'd know my sisters bang the dishes.

So many times, we don't listen and we miss so much. Listen to the leaves swaying back and forth in the wind and to the dogs barking. Just listen. Be still and listen. My point is, that we, your Divine loved ones in Heaven, are with you. We listen to your every word, thought, and more. Our hearing is different, as it is felt as a vibration. Everything, including emotions, words, and thoughts, are felt as vibrations. When you think you hear or feel us, you are feeling our energy vibration, which your Spirit and Soul know very well. We are communicating all the time with our loved ones.

Have you ever felt something or reacted in a certain way to something and then said, "I know you (a loved one in Heaven) are here." Or have you been led to something by your transitioned loved one? I led my mom to a book store so that she would find a book that I knew she would like. She eventually determined it was me and my energy that was present. My mom has learned to listen, to just listen, and then she hears me. She still doubts if what she hears is real at times, but then she knows that our conversation is not something that could have just come from her, and she knows it must be me. The more she listens, the easier it becomes. My vibration is a higher frequency than yours, so I must lower my frequency. And as you open and allow yourself to receive us, then your frequency rises to meet ours. Pretty cool!

Your transitioned loved ones want to communicate with you, guide you, and assist you. We see your pure, true energy and we know your struggles. We guide and assist you when you allow us to. We move obstacles out of your path, place items in your path, bring people to you, and we even play songs to let you know we are fine. My favorite song is "What a Wonderful World" by Louis Armstrong. My loved ones would hear that song play and know it was me and feel peaceful. I placed my soccer medal from eighth grade in the path of a friend to find after I transitioned. She knew exactly who had done it. I wanted her to know that I appreciated her and how much I loved her cooking, especially her delicious meatballs.

My Earth girlfriend, Antoniette, will tell you that I instantly tried to make sure she knew that I was still there. Especially when she was crying. On her first night of finding out that I had transitioned, she was having difficulties believing I was still there. So, I made the lights in her room flicker, objects fall around her, and words repeat back to her by me through my mom to prove that I was there next to her. Even now, I find ways to show her that I am still here. She doubts many times that it's me. She often tries to convince herself that it's all a coincidence. She almost made herself believe that a car just happened to show up at a certain time each morning because the owner probably drives somewhere at that time, but she soon noticed that the car appears whenever she speaks of me. She realized that it was me, my way of telling her, "Good morning," or, "Hi, Babe. I'm right here, and you're not alone in this."

We communicate in all kinds of ways. But it is super cool when you can hear us. Some people quiet their minds through meditation, gardening, music, or deep breathing.

Whatever it takes to quiet your mind. We want to help you and we are always here for you. Our love never leaves because we never left. We are always in your presence whenever you are accepting of us or even when you are not. So listen. Just listen. Call our name, and we are there. Then listen to what you hear, observe what you see, and just know that information can Divinely appear to you. You may think, *Where did that come from?* or *How do I know that?* It is us!

CHAPTER 6

To Be or Not to Be

Most people will live their lives by other people's programs. Many times, unknowingly. What do I mean by this? Well, most people will go to school or work and comply with other's beliefs or commands even when they themselves know that it is not right for them. The information being told by another may not resonate or seem true to them. Each time you comply with something you don't agree with, you become farther away from the truth you initially knew was right for you. Confusing, I know, but important. One must become aware of what is happening to become empowered to say, "I don't agree with this which I am being told to do, as it is not in the best interest for me or true to me."

When you do something not true to you, you feel it in your Soul. It's like living a lie. Now, I know your question, "What do you do?", since you must go to school and you need your job. Well, it's a dilemma. Comply for them or comply for you.

Feeding your Soul is always best even when it may not be the popular move according to others. But who are you living for, them or you? Whose life is it, their life or your life? What do you do when you need your job or you need to go to school? Well, I can't answer that for you, but you can. Ask your inner guidance what is your best move. Then listen. You might hear, "Stick up for your Soul and do not comply," or you might hear, "Share your feelings about complying with not following your truth." If you choose to comply, you have spoken your truth.

Your inner guidance is your guidance connected to Divine Source (God, Angels, guides, etc.) and it will tell you something specific only for you, that provides information that is in your best interest. It might tell you to change jobs. Who knows. Only your inner guidance knows. However, many people will comply with undesirable commands without questioning.

This results in experiencing a difficult path. When you follow your Soul's guidance, you are led down a more pleasant path since it is in alignment with your Soul. Moving from a negative situation (an unfulfilling job or a controlling teacher) could turn out to be a wonderful move to something much better for you. When you experience a negative situation, this could be your Soul pushing you to a better situation that you will be pleased with.

CHAPTER 7

Live for the Day!

Most of you live your life as if tomorrow will always come. When you lose a loved one in the physical world, you wake up to the reality that tomorrow isn't always given.

Tomorrow may not come for some. So live for the day, the minute, the moment. That is all you really have. This moment. Every moment is special. Special to you and special to others. But let's talk about you. What are you doing in each moment to live your life? Are you loving you? Are you creating? Are you helping others? Are you valuing you, valuing your moment? My famous high school quote was, "Life is short, but I am tall." Are you playing every moment tall? A good and quick way to know is to ask yourself how you are feeling. Are you feeling pleasure and happiness, or are you just allowing life to pass you by while you comply to what others want you to do in your moments? Do your moments bring contentment and movement or sadness and stagnation? Is your Soul happy?

During my last year of Earth life, I took many beach trips with friends. I played soccer. I flew a plane. I spent time with my beautiful girlfriend enjoying every moment. Schoolwork and chores were not my favorite ways to spend my moments, and I felt stagnant doing those things and, of course, I sucked at them. But I'm not saying don't do your homework or chores, just find some joy in doing those things so that your moments are enlightening with movement and not stagnation. However, I know it is not always easy to find joy in something you do not care for, but it is not impossible. If your chore is pulling weeds like mine was, you could enjoy the outdoors, nature, and know that what you are doing is a useful task just in case a raging, out-of-control fire comes racing up to your house. My family knows this one well and they are grateful that I took care of all the weeds.

Looking at a chore from a different perspective can make the chore much easier to do. This can be applied to an unpleasant job or anything else you might originally dislike. As you change to a more positive perspective, your vibration rises, your energy moves, and you feel more pleasure so that you are feeling expansive in each moment, which results in you living each moment. However, if something is causing you great grief, then your Soul is telling you that this is not for you and steering you to discover what feels better. When you choose not to listen to your inner guidance, then you continue with stagnation, feeling stuck, unhappy, and more of what you do not desire.

Following your heart is a good way to live your life. Follow where your Soul leads you. This will always include being playful, joyful, and full of contentment. If something is feeling entirely crappy and you've tried changing your perspective with little improvement in your joy, then follow your Soul's nudging to move to what will bring you joy. Always check in with yourself to know how you are feeling and how you are doing with living every moment in joy and contentment.

There are really only two emotions: Love and Fear.

Love and fear are the root to all emotions. Feeling joy is rooted in love. Feeling sadness is rooted in fear. Living from love brings joy, high vibration, movement, fulfillment. Living from fear brings stagnation, struggles, difficulties, and even poor health.

You get to choose. How many moments do you have

left to live in your physical body? How many moments will you choose to live from love or choose to live from fear? Your choice!

Live with love every moment of the day. Live with an open heart to receive all the wonderful blessings the Universe has for you. I wish I knew this Universal concept better when I was in body. My life would have been a whole lot easier. But I am here to help all of you to live the fulfilled lives your Souls desire during your bodies' existence on Earth.

Live your Life.
Live every moment with love
no matter what you are doing,
even chores.

CHAPTER 8

Focus on You

Have you ever wondered why you get depressed, sad, or ill? It is your Soul speaking to you and telling you that everything is not OK. What do you need to change? What is creating or contributing to the sadness? What do you need to let go of and turn over to your Divine helpers to address? When you continue to not listen to your Soul's messages, you move farther away from your true self. You are focusing on what's outside of you, which includes other people, jobs, school, relationships, and not having what you desire instead of focusing on you and your inner being, your inner guidance.

When discontented, ask yourself, "What am I doing or feeling to allow this discontentment in my life?" Then listen. Take out a pen and write whatever flows down from you to the paper. Bring to light the answers, and the answers will set you free. Free from the discontent, the illness, the lack. Once enlightened, make the changes that please the Soul. Just ask your inner guidance what changes you need to make, and then listen and write. Lovingly listen to what you hear, as it will flow from your heart. Focus completely on you, your needs, and your desires. It could be a change, a move, or maybe a new belief.

You will notice that when you lovingly focus on you and your desires, the depression, the lack, or the illness will begin to disappear, unless you want to hang onto it. Many people hang onto unease out of fear. The fear of living without the unease. The fear of moving forward. The fear of the unknown. The fear of trusting the Divine. But know that you are greatness and that your Soul yearns for you to experience joy and peace. Miracles are achieved when you focus on yourself. When you hear and follow your Divine guidance, you will move into alignment with your desires.

You can heal your life by loving yourself. Love energy is the highest vibrational frequency, and you can direct this energy, this frequency, with your intentions to where you want. Increase love in your life by loving everything, including yourself, your body, your ache or pain, your unruly neighbor, your overdrawn bank account, and you will be amazed at how everything shifts and changes for you. Love everything. You deserve the best. You deserve joy. You deserve peace. Focus on you!

CHAPTER 9

Your Life Plan

Did you know you created your life before entering the Earth Realm? Well, you did. Just as I created mine. I created all the people I would meet. The places I would see. The things I would do. I developed it all prior to coming to Earth. I was a new Soul. That means that I had not experienced other realms other than Source (God) energy. Going to Earth was my first incarnation. This isn't so for most Souls, though. Most Souls have reincarnated many times, lived many lifetimes, and sometimes all at once. Doesn't that blow your mind? Let me explain. When a Spirit develops their life's plan, with much guidance I should add, they decide what lessons they want to learn during their lifetime, while living in a certain realm. A realm is like what you call another dimension. Whatever dimension a Spirit chooses to go to, lessons are to be learned, awareness increased, and consciousness expanded so that the Soul can grow and evolve. If the lesson is mastered, the Soul evolves in this area. If the lesson is not mastered, then that lesson is brought into the next incarnation. That's how you get the past life stuff. It's like unfinished business that your Soul will keep pushing you towards and providing opportunities for you to learn, grow, and expand.

Even though a lesson was not mastered in one lifetime, there was still learning and growth that occurred. The lesson will still need to be learned, but no worries; you will get another chance. I had unfinished business when I transitioned back into only Spirit form. My life purpose and plan was to provide light and guidance to all through compassion. Though I did accomplish much of this, I will continue to work on this lesson when I incarnate again.

What I am trying to say is that you created your life plan with what experiences you desired for you, to move you forward on your path to enlightenment and expansion. You do have choices in how to react to learning life lessons. The Soul, which is all-knowing and powerful, as it is purely connected to Source (God) energy, will provide situations to assist you with growth and expansion. When one does not listen to the Soul's messages, the situations created become louder and more intense. Some examples may include: losing a job, accruing an illness, or a disaster might happen. These challenges will lead a person to enlightenment and ultimately expansion.

You have the choice to listen or not listen to your Soul's Divine guidance. You have the choice between the easy road or the difficult road towards enlightenment and expansion. It is up to you. You create for you. Let me explain. For me, I was to learn unconditional love and compassion for all. Obstacles were thrown into my path, known as difficult life events, including my car continually breaking down and some relationship struggles. Many times, I fell into the trap of getting overwhelmed with the Earthly obstacles, and that blurred my vision of my true path and my connection to the Divine. This resulted in not always connecting with the pure Souls of others, as I was here to do, and providing them with unconditional love and compassion. Connecting to another's pure Divine Soul is seeing them without the Earth baggage in their energy field. Earthly baggage is illnesses, struggles, fears, anger, and lack. But instead of focusing on the Divine goodness of others and within myself, I saw the Earthly baggage and I became wrapped up in it and unfocused on what was real. This is where most beings on Earth reside: focused on the Earthly baggage within themselves and within others. But what was real was love. Our Divine selves are only love. Love is all that is real. Focus on only love in yourself and others and watch how your life turns magical. During my next incarnation, I will continue to work on this lesson.

When you return to Source (God) energy, you see all. You see yourself and others only with love and compassion as the Earthly baggage falls away when only in Spirit form. It is like dead weight (Earthly pressures) lifted off you and you are reborn back to your original free Spirit form with great awareness.

Your time to return home (Heaven) was also set by you.

I chose, before my Earth life, to only live eighteen and a half Earth years in body. I chose to learn all that I had learned and to expand all that I did. I had developed Soul Contracts (contracts that are developed between Souls prior to incarnation) with my loved ones to leave at the time I left to also further their growth and expansion. I was not consciously aware of this while in body, but my Soul knew exactly what I had planned.

I planned to enjoy a wonderful Father's Day with family and friends and then to transition the following morning. I transitioned quickly when I lost control of my car and I was ejected. I felt no physical pain. Angels and my grandmother were there to greet me. They told me to trust that all was well and Divinely planned by me.

I struggled at first to adjust due to my close physical connections on Earth. A Spirit guide, named Erik, came to me and helped me. I had so much Divine assistance and I felt enormous love that I soon remembered my Spirit life before I had entered the Earth realm. Like most Spirits who transition back, I wanted to help my loved ones adjust to my new form. I immediately did things to let my loved ones know that I was fine. I made my old cell phone play music. I locked my bedroom door when my dad felt that he needed to give my things away quickly. This prevented his grieving, which led to health issues.

He wanted to give my things away so he and his loved ones on Earth could move forward, but taking care of business prevents the time needed to grieve.

My friends, family, and acquaintances all took my transitioning differently, and I assisted them all. I came to them in dreams. I talked to them. I pointed them to certain insects and animals (butterflies and birds) to let them know I was OK. My mom could hear me well. Even then, however, she did not always trust what she heard. Especially on the night that I passed. She was brushing her teeth, and I told her, "I don't have to brush my teeth anymore."

My mom said, "That's not funny, Jeremy." But she did smile a little.

My closest Earth bonding at the time I transitioned was my beautiful and amazing girlfriend, Antoniette. We had planned to spend our Earthly lives together. I worried about her and I felt her pain and confusion. I came to her in dreams, as she was unable to focus and hear me. I knocked things over. I played familiar songs. I set up obstacles to show her how powerful she was, as she did not always believe in herself. My mom knew that Antoniette would need a car to go to school and to work, as our (mine and Antoniette's) Earth plan was for her to use my car when I left for the Air Force. But now my car was totaled from the car accident. I found her a car and told my mom. My parents drove with her to Orange County, which required them to drive on freeways for over an hour to see the car. Antoniette test drove the car and she loved it.

My mom then drove the car home and immediately

she knew something was wrong. She said to me, "You said this was the right car, a white Honda."

I replied, "True."

My smart mom immediately took the car to a trusted mechanic. She was told that the car had been in an accident and it had lots of problems. The car had to be returned, and Antoniette had to drive the car alone on the freeway for about sixty miles. Antoniette was a new driver and fearful of driving at times, especially on the freeway. But she agreed to drive the car back. Prior to driving back to Orange County, my mom called about another car to see but she was only able to leave a message of our interest.

So Antoniette and my mom ventured back to Orange County. As they drove slowly and cautiously, my mom in one car and Antoniette in the other car, I could strongly feel Antoniette's fears. I comforted her and told her that she could do this, that she could do anything. My mom and Antoniette made it there safely. Antoniette was so relieved when they arrived; she was shaking inside. My arms were around her the entire time.

They left the dealership in Orange County in my mom's car, and on their way home, another car owner called and requested them to come look at his car. They looked at a Toyota Corolla, and my mom felt and knew that it wasn't the right car. See how we Spirits work. We get into your brain. My mom then remembered that I had said to look for a white Honda. Then the salesman asked, "What kind of car are you looking for?"

My mom answered, "A Honda."

The salesman replied, "We have a white Honda back here with low miles and still under warranty."

My mom and Antoniette liked the car because that was the car meant for Antoniette. My mom asked me, "Why did you make us go through this?"

And I responded, "So that Antoniette would know that she is capable of doing anything and that I am always with her comforting and guiding her."

That's not all to the story. Antoniette gets the perfect car for her, but the tire light had an issue. That was me doing it, but it was needed. It was funny to watch my mom and Antoniette meet at the Honda Dealership each Friday, five or six times, trying to fix this problem. I would laugh each time as Antoniette would drive her car each Friday away from the dealership only for the tire light to go on again, usually within a mile from the dealership. Ha! The mechanics could not understand what was happening. My mom said, "Jeremy, you said this is the car. What's the deal?"

I replied, "The car kept you and Antoniette meeting

every Friday for a while because Antoniette and you needed each other for support." After several weeks, Antoniette had a tire blow out and, of course, I was there comforting and guiding her. My awesome mom said to Antoniette that we would meet at the tire store. New tires were installed, and there was no more tire light issue. Believe it or not, this was all Divinely planned, and within the life plans of those involved.

I will always continue to comfort and guide my loved ones. I will always remain close to them. We will plan more lifetimes together in our physical bodies. But for now, I will guide them in my Spirit form, and they will soon realize that I can assist them more than ever now.

Jeremy and Antoniette

CHAPTER **10**

Be All That You Can Be

When you wake up in the morning, what do you think about? Do you think, *It's going to be a good day,* or do you think, *Life sucks?* You might want to live your life wisely during your time on Earth. If you think it is going to be a good day, that is great. You are probably feeling really good and you are actually setting your day to be good as well. The opposite is also true. If you think that life sucks, well, you guessed it, your day will not go very well. What do you want? It's your choice.

I had both types of days when I was in my body on Earth. I tried to have more positive days though. I loved getting up early on school days and driving to Antoniette's house to wake her up. That was starting my day off right. Thinking of someone you love. When you think about not knowing how many days you have left on Earth, wouldn't you want to choose to wake up feeling good each day? Many of us do not think about not having another day to wake up to until that moment hits when your days are gone. Choose to wake up and have a good day. A wonderful day. The best day of your life.

When our mindset is to have a great day, we are the best that we can be. We are happy. Ideas for what to do next flow rapidly to us, such as driving up to Wrightwood Mountains to watch the sunrise, bugging your girlfriend, singing that song, writing that book, skateboarding under the moonlight, or dancing in the rain.

Whatever flows to you. Then follow those ideas that are feeding your Soul and assisting you to evolve. It's a win-win situation.

Be the best that you can be living each and every day as if it could be your last day on Earth.

*Your mind
is a powerful thing.
When you fill it with positive
thoughts. Your life is about
to hit another peak of change.
Take it in you will like it
Love, Jeremy*

*I wrote this to my dad, who was also my soccer coach, only
a few weeks before I transitioned.*

Love Relationships When a Loved One Transitions

This chapter discusses love relationships, including married couples, dating couples, and couples in love. When a loved one transitions, both can feel lost at first. Especially if the transition is unexpected and quick like mine. The love of my life, Antoniette, and I were both in shock. We had Earth plans to have a long Earth life together, and that all changed when I transitioned. I was so sad knowing that I had let her down. She counted on me to always be there. I loved her so much. I still do, and I always will. I received support from Spirit Guides, Angels, Source (God), and loved ones in Heaven, and loved ones on Earth helped Antoniette. It is an adjustment. A big adjustment in which eventually we must let go of what we thought was our plan and follow what now is our plan.

Often our Earth plan is different from our Soul plan. We develop our Soul Plan prior to entering the Earth plane, and our time to leave was already predetermined before being born (as previously stated in Chapter 9). Though I had hints that I was leaving my Earth body soon, I consciously was unaware. I lived my last year of life like it was my last, doing all the things I wanted to do, as I was thinking that I was leaving for the Air Force. I would say, "You only live once." My point is that our departure time is predetermined. The Souls of our loved ones are aware of our time to transition as well, and they have agreed to this contract to learn the lessons they came to Earth to learn.

Since I left my body, Antoniette has grown into an independent and powerful person. Her growth and expansion has been amazing, and I cheer her on every step of the way. I know that it hasn't been easy, but I am so proud of her. These changes may not have occurred so quickly if I were still there in body.

But what is our relationship like now? Antoniette's energy is always connected to mine. I comfort her when she is sad and I cheer her up, making her laugh, when she is frustrated or angered. I even flicker the lights when her boss is not kind.

Couples in real love stay connected even when one leaves their body. After I left the Earth plane, Antoniette was confused and didn't want to date again. In time that will change, as Earth beings find comfort, joy, and peace with the companionship of another.

Companionship is important for growth on Earth. Antoniette felt that she would lose me if she opened her heart up to another love relationship. I told her she would not lose me, as we will always be connected in some way. However, those remaining on Earth must release some of the connectedness so that they are open to receive all the goodness Earth has to offer, including other love relationships.

Our (us in Heaven) relationships with loved ones on Earth changes. Many of us become guides to assist our loved ones in the different dimensions. So the question is, "Is it okay for our Divine loved ones in Heaven and for our loved ones on Earth to love again?" The answer is, "Yes! Yes! Yes!" We want that. Your loved ones in Heaven do not get jealous or upset. We want our loved ones to experience all that life on Earth has to offer, including more than one love relationship on Earth. Intimate love relationships are never forgotten.

No worries there. However, you must release some of your energy that is connected to us. That might include memories and desires so that new memories and desires can be created.

Loved ones in Heaven must do the same so that we can continue to expand and grow as well. We do this through changes and not holding onto past energy. In a close relationship, the love is so great that you want, no matter what, for your partner to be happy. When we in Heaven see our loved ones smiling and living happily, we are smiling too.

Some couples made contracts to join their loved ones in Heaven soon after their loved one's transition. But for most, this is not the case. A loved one's transition is for expansion and growth for all involved. In Heaven (Home), you have loving feelings towards all so we hope that you choose to live your lives to the fullest with loving relationships included. We choose this in Heaven as well. Love is what it's all about!

CHAPTER 11

All Is Divinely Planned

When a loved one transitions, many people have regrets. They ask themselves: *What should I have done? What could I have done? What didn't I do? What shouldn't I have done?* My mom regrets not attending my tennis matches, not spending more time with me, and not trying harder to get along with me when I was being a jerk. She held onto this for months after I transitioned even when I told her it was all Divinely perfect. I, too, felt sadness over not doing things I thought that I should have done, not hugging my family more, and not being a better son. But all is Divinely perfect.

Prior to coming to a planet, we create our Soul Contracts within our life plans. This contract, as previously mentioned, contains what lessons we will learn, what people we will meet, and what we will do. All participants in our "planet experience" have agreed to participate and assist in learning and expansion for us. This is a contract to help them to learn, grow, and expand as well. With that being said, my mom played her role in my Earthly life perfectly so that I was able to learn, grow, and expand in all the ways that I did.

My mom chose to have five kids. When my twin sisters came along, four years after I was born, my sisters took up much of my mom's time. I would say that I was spoiled rotten until my sisters arrived, and though my mom provided me love, I wanted more. My dad was awesome, and he and I were tight. But I wanted more of my mom's attention. I began to ignore the many ways she was there for me and loved me. I focused on not having her when I wanted her. As I became older, especially my last year of Earth life, I distanced myself more from my mom. This was Divinely planned and perfect; my mom and I played our roles perfectly to both learn what we came to Earth to learn.

My mom always loved me, even when I was a jerk. She learned to look beyond the surface behavior and to connect on a Soul level. This was a life lesson for her, and I played my role perfectly. I learned to find the love and attention I desired in other ways. I loved my friends and I connected with them on a deep level. My lesson to learn was to connect with other Souls by looking beyond surface behaviors. I saw my friends for who they really were and assisted them in being themselves.

My point is that my mom had to be the way she was and I had to be the way I was so that we both could learn, grow, and evolve. No regrets. It was all perfectly orchestrated by and for those involved. It is awesome to learn and expand our awareness, accomplishing what we go to a planet to accomplish. Let those regrets go and live. Everything that occurred was necessary for expansion. I thank my mom, my friends, and my family for being the way they were, which assisted me in my expansion. I appreciate all my experiences and I appreciate everyone who played a part in them, and so should you.

CHAPTER 12

Forgiving Will Set You Free!

Sometimes to let emotions, like regret, go we must apologize to others, forgive others, and especially forgive ourselves. On Earth, we feel that everyone is judging us, but it is really us judging ourselves. We can be our own worst enemies and we can be hard on ourselves, not forgiving ourselves. No Divine beings, God, our Source, Angels, or Spirits ever judge us or anyone. All is just as it is, which is perfect for learning and growth.

I have a story about my emotional growth. I told my mom after my passing that I was sincerely sorry for being difficult during my last year on Earth. I felt terrible for what I caused. I was also judging myself. As soon as I apologized to my mom and forgave myself,

I felt a weight lift from me. My Spirit was freed and able to grow and to expand more. It was funny because my mom had already let go of any anger or resentment she had previously carried, but the self-recrimination and the pain I felt continued deep in my Soul until I apologized and completely let it go.

This happens on Earth; we carry around so much emotional baggage that it weighs us down. Often the emotional baggage comes from being hurt by another or from guilt over hurting someone. Many times, the other people involved have already let it go. But for many of us, we continue to hold onto emotional baggage until we decide to make a conscious choice to let it go. Forgiving yourself and forgiving others is freeing to you. It is sad when people choose to not forgive another or even forgive themselves because they themselves are the ones that suffer. They hold onto the anger and hurt, and that eats away on a Soul level. And for what? Why would you do that to yourself? The other person is fine, probably forgot about the incident that occurred and has moved on with their life. If people on Earth could see on the energetic level like I can, they would see the damage these emotional wounds cause; everyone would let their emotional baggage go. It's not worth it.

When you forgive someone, you are not forgiving

the inappropriate act; you are forgiving the person and choosing to see him or her through compassionate eyes. You see the pain they experienced and you develop an understanding of what led up to an unkind act. We are all God's children and Divine beings of love. Life experiences occur and can mask that loving Divine person. This results in that person behaving in a poor manner, but they are still Divine love and they are still a child of God. When you view Earth life from our Divine position in Heaven, you will see that all is and was Divinely planned for all involved to learn, grow, and to expand consciousness.

Return to love, loving all, loving everything, even the "what appears negative" so that you learn, do, and feel what you came to Earth to experience. Express gratitude for your emotional baggage and let it go. Free yourself. Live your life just as you had planned it, flowing through the ups and downs by forgiving and then releasing the energy that is not helping you.

When you do this, then you will be living in love and joy!

CHAPTER 13

You Are the Artist for Your Life

All is Divinely planned. You are the artist and the creator of your life. I know you are thinking, *What is Jeremy talking about?* I touched on this a bit earlier. In your Soul Plan, which you made before coming to Earth, you developed circumstances that would assist you in learning, growing, and expanding in the areas you chose to expand in.

You had lots of assistance in developing your plan, and others agreed to assist you in growing since you had agreed to assist them as well.

We all want to expand. We want to expand our awareness, our knowledge, our consciousness, and our existence. That is what you are on Earth to do, I am in Heaven to do, and we all exist to do. To grow. To expand. To evolve.

As we develop our Soul Plan and contracts, we may desire to grow in self-love so we will paint like an artist, or write the scene of a play to assist us in loving our self. In her Soul Plan my mom wrote circumstances to help her learn self-love. She had a contract with a Soul friend to enter her life at a time that she had requested to learn this life lesson of self-love. This friend had agreed to play this part. After having no contact with this friend for over thirty years, the friend contacts her and she immediately felt a magnitude of self-hate. Self-hate for how she was. Self-hate for how she looked. An overwhelming amount of self-hate. Just major self-hate. For her to truly feel self-love, she had to feel the opposite. This is the polarity that you have on Earth. So as my mom struggled on her journey at that time in her life, confused most times but knowing she would succeed, she experienced ailments, weight loss, relationship problems, and more. However, she always kept searching for answers in healing and peace. She chose to experience this lesson on a very deep level. As she witnessed herself aging quickly due to the stress involved, this created self-sabotage and extreme hatred towards herself. But there was a point in all this that she chose to experience and she continues to rise above. My mom is an Angel who chose to come to Earth to experience Earth life personally. This life would consist of hardships and struggles to help her develop empathy on a deep level, which is necessary to assist others on their own journeys.

We all create our own experiences to expand and evolve. My journey on Earth was complete for that lifetime when I left. I was what is known as an Indigo Child, sent to Earth to assist in change and bring peace. I was closely connected with Divine forces, as you all are, to progress on my journey. I planted seeds in people. I gave encouragement and love so they knew they were important. I loved them so they knew they could accomplish anything they wanted. I had Divinely planned my Earth life just as every Spirit does. In addition, I Divinely planned my exit to occur on a Strawberry Moon and Summer Solstice and to have an immediate exit with no others physically hurt from the car accident. It was all Divinely planned, and my three buddies in my car at the time of the accident had agreed to assist with my exit. They did not know this on a conscious level, but their Souls were aware of it. My Soul was aware of my exiting from my body as well, but I was not consciously aware of any of this. It took a short while to adjust back to Home, but I had wonderful assistance. You will learn more about this in the next chapter. See you there.

CHAPTER 14

Returning Home

When I transitioned, I was first greeted by my grandmother who had transitioned four months earlier. She was waiting for me. She comforted me and, dang, I was really confused. I worried about my girlfriend, my family, my friends, but mostly my girlfriend. I connected with my mom right away and knew she would try to bring peace to it all. She had been preparing for a tragic event for over a year without knowing exactly what it was to be. She thought it would be a flood or an earthquake. She had contact with her Heavenly guides, one of whom was Mother Mary, who told her to assist and inform that all was Divinely well and to have faith in our Maker when the tragedy hit. My mom believed that all was well, as Mary had said, and she exhibited great faith as she went through her grieving.

My heart broke, and I was sad to watch my loved ones suffer. I received guidance, support, and reassurance that I would still always be connected to my loved ones. I began to remember the Soul Contracts with loved ones that we all had agreed on and the lessons we all agreed to learn. I saw that all was Divinely orchestrated for us and by us in the loving arms of our wonderful Source (God). I comforted my loved ones and held them tight as they grieved and expanded in the way they had desired to expand from this experience.

I also gave signs that I was well. My mom saw a yellow butterfly. She said it was beautiful. She saw it at home, at the Wrightwood Mines that I loved to visit, and at a soccer game that my sisters played in. They just happened to play their soccer game on field number twelve. The number twelve was my jersey number when I played soccer and it's my favorite number. My mom picked up on this coincidence right away. My sisters won that tournament, and the team received a large rock as a trophy. They had never seen a trophy like that before, and my mom thought of me right away. She thought the trophy looked like a tombstone. She knew it was me who had intended for it to look like that and said, "Good one, Jeremy."

The rock trophy Jeremy's mom referred to as a tombstone.
"Good one, Jeremy."

Jeremy's number twelve.

My reason for returning Home was that I completed my mission on Earth and I knew that I could assist more Souls in their own expansion if I did so in my Spirit form from Home. I had so much support when I returned Home that adjusting did not take long. It is difficult to hold a low vibration of sadness when you are surrounded by so much love.

CHAPTER 15

What I Do Now

My mission on Earth was to enlighten, assist, and grow. I accomplished all I was there to accomplish. I taught people to be themselves, their true selves, without all the Earthly baggage, which is just fear. Without fear, there is only love, and that is what you are. I assisted in reminding them by my actions and my words to be themselves. I also made myself grow in amazing ways. I didn't realize how much I evolved until I returned Home and I could see the effects my being on Earth played for myself and for others' journeys. It was amazing to see.

Being at Home (Heaven), I continue to assist, grow, and expand in consciousness. I comfort and assist all my loved ones on Earth and I comfort and assist Souls as they are transitioning to Earth. Earth is not an easy planet to exist on, but it is well worth the travel. The growth and expansion is amazing. That is why so many Souls choose Earth to visit. They can evolve more quickly on Earth. Our roles at Home are just as important as our roles on other planets. We are always growing, expanding, and evolving towards being like our Source or God energy. Your Souls know exactly what I am talking about. So as Spirits and Souls transition from Home to another realm or planet, I comfort, support, and guide them as they adjust to their transition. It is not always an easy transition, but it occurs just as they planned it, and they evolve just as they wanted to.

Some Souls choose difficult births, and their physical bodies experience pain right away. The more difficulties experienced, the greater expansion and growth their Souls can receive. Many choose very difficult Earth lives so to evolve more quickly.

Mahatma Gandhi and Adolf Hitler are examples of a quick transformative journey. That's right, Hitler too. He was playing his role, as cruel as he appeared to others, perfectly to evolve more quickly. All those affected by Hitler agreed prior to incarnating to be a part of his evolution. They evolved greatly as well. When something devastating occurs on Earth, remember it is and was Divinely planned by all involved. This is what we do. We learn, grow, expand, and evolve whether you are on Earth or at Home. By the way, your Spirit visits Home all the time, especially when you sleep.

My role or my job is to remind people who they are. My mom is stepping into this as well, as her role is to do the same.

She loves sharing God's Divine energy to help people along their journeys. Crystals, oils, and nature are her favorites, and they all assist with remembering who we are: perfect and Divine beings. She comes to you on Facebook, in person, and on the internet. I come to you in your dreams, your thoughts, and your knowing. Trust your knowing. You know all this that I have shared. All of it.

For those getting ready to transition to planets, I set up signs, obstacles, and incidents with them to remind them who they really are when they forget. Everything is Divinely planned for you, for your growth and expansion. Everything is Divinely perfect. Everything. All situations just are for our growth. Trust what you know by letting go of resistance. Letting go of fear. Fear of being your true self. Fear is resistance. This will open you up to you, which is love. It is amazing how after you let go of fear, ailments, depression, relationship issues, and lack, they will all disappear. This is because you are now living in love, with abundance and extreme gratitude for all that occurs.

Expand, love, evolve, and be the best that you are. You are already Divinely the best. You are!

CHAPTER **16**

How to Thrive When You Miss Your Loved Ones in Heaven

Cry. Let it out. Climb a mountain. Scream. Cry. We are holding you as you mourn. It is extremely important to let it out. Holding on to grief and sorrow causes all kinds of problems including deep depression and ailments. Let it out. Feel the pain and let it go. Don't live in the pain. That is not living. I know it can be difficult to understand that we did not go anywhere except to transition into only our Spirit form. We stay with our loved ones. We guide them. We assist them. We give comfort and support. Soon you will be in Spirit form only, just like us, but for now you are in your body to live. To live. To live your life to the fullest, and we both know that life cannot be lived to the fullest if you are stuck in grief.

When you want to hug us, hug someone close to you, and you will feel us hugging you. We hug you all the time. Your Spirit and Soul know that. When you remember something about us while we were on Earth, smile and know we had fun. All is good once a Spirit transitions out of body. Even the bad times are understood, like when your loved one in Heaven was mean or hurt someone while in body. Well, now it is understood that he was just having a bad day. This will happen for you this way too. All is good and understood and forgiven. All is how it is supposed to be.

Smile when you remember us. We are smiling with you. But if a flood of tears comes rushing in, let them flow and know that we are holding you and comforting you. Allow the tears to release instead of holding onto them so you can return to living your life fully in happiness and joy. You are on your own mission on Earth, just as I was. A mission to learn, to grow, and to evolve. Focus on your mission and know that we can help by guiding you and giving you support.

Love yourself enough to know that you deserve to live your life on Earth in joy and in peace. It does not hurt our feelings when you do not think about us every day. That shows us that you are living your life. Our Spirits are always communicating. Release all fears that you might forget about us or lose us if you don't always think about us. This isn't going to happen. We both agreed prior to our Earth lives to stay connected for a long time. A long time and many times for eternity. No worries. Live. Live your life.

Find your joy and do more of that. This is what God wants for all of us. We are well cared for here in Heaven and we are surrounded by only loving Souls, many who we have known for lifetimes. When we feel sad, it is short lived. Sadness is a low vibration and it becomes overpowered quickly by the higher vibrations of love and joy. Remember, emotions are felt in vibrations. Earth doesn't hold the higher vibrations (love and joy) consistently like in Heaven, but you can choose to hold the higher vibrations for yourself while on Earth. Choose to experience the high vibrations of love, joy, and gratitude, and then the lower vibrations of sadness, guilt, and resentment disappear.

You choose your life. Try to not view someone transitioning into pure Spirit form as a loss. View it as transforming and returning Home to the familiar. Familiar Souls, Spirits, our Source or God. It is a celebration of completing our Earthly tasks and Earthly evolution. A job well done. An accomplishment. We are rewarded and then can continue to help those in body, but on a larger scale and quicker. We visit so many Souls and Spirits all at once and provide what is needed at that time if they are open. The Soul and Spirit are open, but often the ego is not. The ego can get stuck in disempowering beliefs and remain closed to our support, not wanting to grow. The ego lives in fear. The Spirit and Soul live in love. A person must be willing and open to receive our support. It is a choice.

When a person is in a low vibration energy of grief and sadness, it is difficult to receive our help, as our energies are on a very different vibrational level. But you get to choose which vibrational level you would like to be on by the thoughts and beliefs that you have. Sad thoughts trap you. Thoughts of joy and gratitude release you and open you/open you up and allow you to receive. An example of a good thought to choose when grieving for a loved one is, *I am sad, and I miss my boy in body, and I choose to be joyful and happy and to live a wonderful and fulfilled life.*

Acknowledge your sadness and then use the word *and* to choose how you want to feel. This will keep the energy flowing and eliminate stuck energy that will cause you problems.

It's a choice to live in grief or to live in joy. We hope

that you choose joy, as your time on Earth will quickly fly by, and we know you want to expand and to grow as much as possible while you are in your body on Earth. It's a choice. What do you choose? We always support you and your journey no matter what you choose, and we are happy when you choose to move through life's circumstances gracefully and with gratitude rather than to provide yourselves with additional struggles that you create on your journey.

To put it simply, focus on love and gratitude and everything will fall into place. Love and gratitude for your loved ones' presence on Earth and for those present in Heaven. Focus on love and gratitude for your loved ones' presence on Earth more gracefully. Love is familiar to your Soul, as you are love. You were created by Source energy or God, and so you are a part of God energy. And since God is love, so are you!

CHAPTER 17

Your Gifts

You all have special Divine gifts that you transitioned to Earth with. Some of you sing. Some dance, draw, or maybe golf. It's what you love to do. Your gifts are what you love and enjoy doing. When you express and share your gifts, your heart sings, all things seem right, and you smile from ear to ear. Some may think, *I don't know what my gifts are.* Then ask yourself, what do you love to do? Ride motorcycles, ski, or make sandcastles while playing in the sand? Our gifts are all unique. One's gift might be to make candles and another might share the same gift of making candles. But the candles that both people make will be different because everyone is uniquely different along with their gifts.

When you focus on what you love and what brings you joy (your gifts), you can profit from sharing your gifts with others. Our unique gifts are sought out by others. Others are waiting for your gifts to surface and to experience them. And you can be rewarded with money for sharing your unique gifts. Take, for example, a person whose gift is golf. They are good at golfing. People want to watch them golf. They win golf tournaments displaying their gift. They write a book titled *Learning to Golf 101*. They assist in teaching others to golf well. They are rewarded handsomely for sharing their gift. They are living in joy, sharing of themselves and helping others. That is Divine. Divine living. The Divine you.

You are all Divine, but many go through their lifetime not sharing their gifts. My gift while on Earth was to bring harmony, make others laugh, and assist others to live their true Divine selves. My friends knew that I didn't take any nonsense from teachers, parents, or anyone else. They saw that I lived my true Divine self doing what I knew to be true and right for me and not what others thought was right for me. Others learned from my behavior to live from their Divine selves and to not take nonesense either. What I am saying is you know your true Divine self and your

Divine gifts. Don't let anyone sway you or tell you that you are not what you know yourself to be and that your gifts are different than what you know they truly are. You are the only one who knows about you.

I also had a gift of flying planes. I loved to fly. It brought me joy. I had Earth plans of flying for the Air Force and flying my friends and family around. I loved my gift. My family supported my gift, and it brought me so much joy. I would have profited from this gift financially, but my time on Earth was up. However, I did profit from my gift of flying on so many levels, including fulfillment, freedom, love for my life, enjoyment, and feeling limitless. I knew I was limitless in what I could accomplish with flying, and I loved all my support.

Support from others on Earth is awesome, but you don't always have that. An example would be if your parents want you to be a doctor, but your true gifts are surfing and teaching others to surf. Surfing is what brings you joy. When this happens, remember you have all the support and guidance you need within you already. Divine guidance and support is greater than any outside support anyways. Your loved ones mean well, but they are living from their dream and not yours. It is sad if you get to the end of your life and you have not shared yourself or your gifts with the world.

Follow your dreams, sharing your gifts,
and you will be eternally rewarded!

CHAPTER 18

Love You

God loves you. The Angels love you. So you need to love you. You are amazing. You are beautiful. You are the only you. There is no one else like you. You are unique, the one and only. There is no one that looks like you, thinks like you, feels the things that you feel. No one. So why do people stop loving themselves? Because they listen to others and what others believe about them. They listen to the negativity, such as, "You're too slow," "You're always sick," "You're too thin or too fat." You are this and you are that; and you believe that which you hear.

Would God and the Angels ever tell you something negative about you? Heck no! They love you. They are love, and you are their (God and the Angels) energy, so why would they? God and the Angels would never say anything negative about themselves. God and Angels are enlightened to know better. Negative thoughts and comments only move you farther away from your God self, which is love. You create you. When you feed into the comments you hear, including, "You're not good enough," "You're unlovable," or "You're too fat," then that is what you create for you. Yes, you create that for you. You will indeed become fat, unlovable, or whatever you believe.

Hear me on this! You create you from whatever you believe. I know we already discussed this, but it is important. The good thing about knowing this concept is you can create the you that you love. The beautiful you that you love with the perfect body weight, the energetic you, the you that loves all and loves you. God, the Angels, and your loved ones in Heaven can assist you in creating the you that you love. But you must request for Divine help, as we cannot step in unless you ask. You are all on your own journey to learn what you have chosen to learn in your lifetime, and we are not able to assist unless you request our assistance. We lovingly comfort and support all that you desire.

But back to loving you. How do you do this when you have years of not loving you? Possibly even years of hating you. How do you love you? Start by acknowledging something about you that you like, your eyes, your hair, your memory, your niceness, your singing, whatever it might be, and start with that. Love that which you have chosen. Love it big. Focus on it. Focus on it a lot. Tell yourself how much you love your eyes. Say something such as, "I love my beautiful blue eyes that see all." Stare into the mirror and express how much you love your eyes. Do these many times a day. Write and place notes around to remind you to focus on that which you love. Say it out loud. When you accomplish this, you are focusing on that which you love. You are transforming your belief system to focus on what you love instead of the dislikes you have about yourself. These dislikes are just beliefs you obtained from others' beliefs and comments about you. This thinking process will grow the you that you love. It transforms you. Continue to do this until you love every aspect of you. Focusing on only that which you love will make everything else non-loving disappear.

How do you feel when you love yourself? Wonderful, right? How do you feel when you are not loving you? Probably horrible. Which do you choose for your life on

Earth? That which brings you joy? Or that which brings you pain? It's your life and choice! Live it while loving you and watch all the beautiful things you attract come your way.

Love You!
You are Beautiful!

CHAPTER 19

Live Free

Live free as a bird or free as a tiger. Live without confinements. Live free. Don't limit yourself with beliefs. Beliefs are only beliefs. They are not real. All that is real is love. Beliefs place limits on you. Examples of a belief might be, "I get sick when I fly," "I will get fat if I eat that cake," "I will get hit by a car if I walk late at night," "I will have heart problems like my father and his father." These are all just beliefs. Perhaps you might want to eat healthy for your body to function well or take a flashlight when walking in the dark, but your beliefs will attract those things that you give attention to. Let's take, for instance, the belief: "I will get fat if I eat that cake." You could be eating a salad, but because your belief is you will get fat, then it is highly likely you will get fat. "Why?" you ask. Because you are focusing on the belief, "You will get fat if you eat that cake," or salad, or whatever food you are focusing on. When you focus on something, the Divine Universe thinks that is what you want, so it is delivered to you. Our negative beliefs have the capability of limiting us and materialize what we do not want.

You are a child of the highest God and you are limitless. That means that you can have anything that you desire if it is in your highest and best good. Anything. God can make all things possible. We are all part of God, so we, ourselves, can make all things possible for us. Pretty cool! It's time to stop limiting ourselves and our dreams. It's time to obtain that which is truly ours. It's time to step up and address our current beliefs and question if our beliefs are serving us or not. It's time to return to our limitless thinking.

How do you do this? Reflect on one of your beliefs and write down how it limits you. An example belief is, "I have anxiety attacks so I cannot socialize with others." The limits in this belief are that you might keep to yourself, not connect with others, and not attend desired functions. The list goes on. Now you get to decide if this is a belief that you would like to keep or not. Does this belief assist you in growing and feeling expansive? Or does it keep you stuck and feeling frustrated? It's your choice. You have choices in your life. Do you want to choose the safe and familiar belief that will keep you stuck? Or do you choose the unlimited belief, such as, "I am confident and safe wherever I go." How do you feel after saying that statement?

What do you choose to believe in? To think unlimited will probably feel uncomfortable at first because it is something new and you are not used to it yet. But the more you choose unlimited, the easier this choice becomes, the freer you become, and the more this will resonate with you. To be limitless is truly how you are designed to be. You can do anything. You deserve everything. Everything is within your reach. Reach high. Live free. Live the true unlimited you and enjoy your life by bestowing gratitude for the Divine you every day you are on Earth.

Dream Big!
Live Big!
You are Limitless!

CHAPTER 20

Judgments

Judging. Why do we judge? Are we feeling bad about ourselves so we become concerned with other's judgments? Do we sometimes think that we know what's best for someone else and for their life? Yes, we are not feeling good about ourselves when we judge! Judging begins with you and how you are feeling about you. Only you know about you, and the same is true for others. So why judge?

Some believe it makes them feel better to judge others, but does it really? Since we are not living other's lives, we cannot judge what is best for them. When one judges another, they are in fact judging themselves. Yep, really! So, when you see someone and think, "Why are they eating that high-calorie food? They are so big and they will get bigger," in truth you are concerned about your own weight and diet. Why? Because you know you and they know them. You know what is best for you, and they know what is best for them.

When you judge and you don't listen to your own judgmental comments, you move farther away from you (yourself). This is because your attention is on another's energy and not yours. The message you were giving to another through judgment was actually for you. You are helping you if you choose to understand the process that is taking place and you direct your energy to focus back only on you. It is then you can ask yourself, "What is it about my diet or weight that I'm unhappy with?" Maybe you need to have a healthier diet to have the ideal weight you would like.

Unfortunately, giving your focus and energy to others by judging is your ego trying to keep you safe. Your ego diverts your focus outside of yourself with the intention of missing your Divine messages that move you forward in your desires. In the ego's attempt to try and keep you safe, you get stuck in your comfort zone of focusing outside of yourself (by judging others), and this is not living. When one is focusing on another, it isn't always easy to make the choices we know we need to make for ourselves since we are distracted and involved in another's energy. Judging is a waste of time unless you want to stay stuck and confined.

It's all a choice. Choose. Whatever you choose, your Divine guidance is there to support, comfort, and guide. But we love when those on Earth pick a choice of least resistance and moves them more gracefully through Earth life. Earth has many distractions, and judging is one of them. Our egos tend to judge ourselves as well, to keep us safe, but stuck. Your ego (which is usually heard as a small voice) will say you are overweight, and you might think unhealthy thoughts. The ego does not have nice things to say about you.

One can distinguish between ego thoughts and Divine thoughts. Divine thoughts are always positive, loving, and uplifting. For example, you might hear or have a knowing that your body is love and perfect. That you are guided to value yourself by choosing to eat a healthy diet, exercising, and allowing the accepted, positive, Divine thoughts to flow to you. Ego thoughts are the opposite; they are not loving. You might hear the ego say you are fat and need to exercise. Exercise is good, but paired with the degrading thoughts, you might over-exercise or diet too much, which can be destructive to you.

When doing all things, come from your Divine self,

from your heart, with only love. Love you, listen to the steps your Divine guidance gives you, and do them. It's all in love. Know that the ego will fight you on this, trying its best to keep you stuck. But remember that you are a Divine being. You are here to grow and to experience life. The ego is from this Earth. The ego is not who you are. Follow your heart, as this is the Divine you, the you that has all the answers for you to advance in your Divine life of only love. Judging only hurts you. Yep! Move past that and live from you!

CHAPTER 21

You Design You

Did you know you designed yourself before going to Earth? Yes, that's right. You designed every aspect of yourself, including your hair color, your eyes, your nationality, the way you walk, the way you talk, the bumps and bruises you will obtain, and when you will obtain them. You orchestrated you and your life prior to coming to Earth.

When we transition back to Heaven (or Home), we start designing our life for our next lifetime. We devise every aspect of it. We have Divine assistance throughout the entire process just as you did. You designed you and your life by the lessons you wish to learn and achieve. By achieve, I mean evolve, which is to shift and move closer to your true Divine self (which many call God).

All lessons learned in life lead us to expanding the God-self in all of us. Cool!

So how can this knowledge help you? You know those times when you get stuck in life and Angelic beings come to help you? That is real stuff. Those Divine beings on Earth and in Heaven create what is necessary in the experiences that are presented to you so you can learn the lessons you chose to learn. Quiet your mind and be present with yourself. You will know that what I have shared is entirely truthful.

With all this being revealed, I don't want you to feel helpless on Earth knowing all was previously planned, because you continue to orchestrate your life on Earth. "How?" you ask. By listening to yourself and following your desires. Just as you designed you prior to your Earth experience, designing you resumes on the Earth plane. You continue to design you, your life, your situations, your everything. For example, Divine guidance continues when you are in body on Earth. It communicates mostly with your Spirit because your Spirit is always open and able to hear and receive.

All is always well. Know that all is well. Seek answers from the inside and not from the outside when venturing on your journey. What others on Earth say is not always what is best for you. You are always Divinely connected to your Source or your God. Always! Your perfect answers come from Source.

Searching for answers outside of you is a waste of time. No one knows you like your Source, as you are Source energy or God energy.

You design you, including designing your body. When you want to lose weight, don't design yourself by looking outward for the answers to lose weight, such as diets, doctors, or weight-control clinics. Instead, look inward towards your Source energy to design yourself and your ideal weight with Source's assistance. If you choose, you can design yourself thin. Connect with Source energy to obtain your special instructions to do that. It is different for everyone; everyone is so unique and perfect already. We merely choose not to see ourselves as perfect.

Look within. Listen and do. Act on what you hear, feel, see, and know. This is your Divine guidance assisting you in designing you. You are on Earth to play with this feature called designing. Designing you. Designing your life. Designing your world. If you choose, you can design a cool red car to drive and a dream house to live in. You can design yourself as a millionaire or a doctor. You can design good health. You design all that you want, good or bad. Technically there is no bad, only learning lessons to steer you back to what you call good. And yes, you also design your learning lessons.

Design what you wish for your life by connecting to Source energy and receive the metaphorical blueprints needed for your design. Then do what Source or God says. You will be happy you did. Trust me on this!

Happy Designing!

CHAPTER 22

Do You Believe in Angels?

I do, I did, and I always have. My mom is an Angel, and I guess by being so close to an Angel in my Earth life, I remained close to Angels. Angels are all around us. There are Angels from above and Earth Angels in physical form with you. They guide and assist in whatever we do. They hold and comfort us when we are sad. Angels are pure light, wisdom, and joy.

They see where we have been, where we are, and what is ahead. Angels pave the way for us when we allow them to.

You must request their assistance and then allow for their help. Angels can only intervene when you request. Otherwise, they must step back and show you they are present by the signs they place for you. They will always step in when you are ready for their help by making your request. They continually show you signs by placing feathers on your path, playing inspiring songs, placing shiny pennies where you walk, and whispering in your ear. They provide comfort all the time by holding your hand and massaging your back. In emergency situations, they bring assistance for help. All Angels support every one of you on your journey. They love you very much.

Angels constantly talk to you attempting to lead you down a path of least resistance, which is a more joyful path. They shine their light from above.

Our Archangels have specific jobs to perform.

Archangel Michael protects us. His light is purple and blue. Archangel Raphael helps heal us, and his light is a yellowish light green. Archangel Haniel assists in helping one remember their true Divine self. Her light is a golden Divine color. The Angels want you to call on them always, to assist, guide, and support in all that you do.

How do you call on Angels? Knowing they are already there with you, calling is easy. Call them by name or request an Angel to come or appear to you. You can ask for the name of the Angel when you feel their presence if you like, but this is not necessary. However, you must request what type of assistance you would like from the Angels, whether it is to release you from sorrow, pain, and anger, or comfort you as you mourn. They do it all. You can request anything, and it is never a bother to them. They love you so much and have only Divine care and support for you.

Angels can assist with decisions to make, such as a business you want to pursue or a relationship you desire. You can request and ask them anything, and it will be done if your request is in your highest and best interest. Their assistance will come to you at the perfect moment. The perfect moment may not be the moment you requested, but it will be the perfect moment for you. Remember, they see your energy and know what the best timing is for you. Once you make your request, give thanks. Angels enjoy gratitude and feeling your love. Then wait. See what comes to you. Answers can appear in a dream, by running into a certain person, on TV or radio, or just a Divine knowing of what to do next can magically appear. Angels move us closer to our true selves. All your activities, your desires, and your pleasures are moving you back to you. The you with amazing health, wealth, prospering business, loving relationships, joy, and peace.

The only thing you need to do is to follow the Angels' Divine guidance that you receive. Then, what you desire will appear in the perfect time if it is for your highest and best interest. But many miss this step of receiving. They do not move past their situation because they do not implement the Divine guidance that they received from the Angels. They chose not to act on the information provided by the Angels or they may have doubted the information they were told. That is okay though, because the Angels will continue to comfort and support you.

When you are ready to follow their Divine lead, they are cheering you on and providing the light on your path. You will see Angel signs often (feathers, coins, consecutive numbers), confirming their presence and support. You are loved so much by the Angles, and they are always there for you in whatever you desire, so don't forget about them. They love when you call them for assistance.

My mom found it helpful to communicate with the Angels using Angel cards. Angel cards assist when your mind is cluttered and unfocused, causing difficulty in hearing the Angels. The messages you receive from the Angel cards are chosen just for you by the Angels. This is a direct method to obtain assistance from the

Angels and a perfect way to begin your communication with them. My mom loves Angel Cards, and any Angel Card deck will provide the perfect message you need to hear at that moment. Angel cards are easy to use, and you can't read them wrong. Why not? The Angels are monitoring the cards and picking the very best one just for you.

Connecting with the Angels makes Earth Life much easier. You always know and feel someone has your back in all situations. You're more daring in taking those steps that may seem scary or difficult. Having that strong Divine connection with the Angels brings joy, peace, and an instinct that everything is perfect. Everything is perfect and well. Enjoy connecting with the Angels. As my mom always says, "Angel Blessings."

CHAPTER 23

Practice Patience

Have patience and know that all will work out. Patience in knowing that all that occurs is Divine and necessary for your growth. You cannot hurry the Divine, because the Divine has your best interest at heart. The Divine plans every step and occurrence out perfectly so you rise above your circumstance in love, honor, and peace. You assisted Divine beings in planning your Earth life to attract and learn lessons that you chose to learn as previously shared. Impatience deters that learning. Impatience slows down growth. Nonetheless, all is good since there is learning in all events.

Love is patient. Love is Divine. Love yourself enough to give yourself the patience you desire to grow.

Trust that the Divine has your back when situations appear out of order, incorrect, or don't seem in your best interest. For example, if a baby is ill and in pain, we may instantly rush to the doctor for support. Many times, the doctor will diagnose the baby with a cold and prescribe medication, not for the baby, but just to comfort you so you feel as though you are helping the baby. When in fact, most medicines will not assist with healing, but only mask the problem or cover it up. Not to say all medicines are unhelpful, but most are. The baby chose their life path, their journey, and they chose their experiences. Many times, medication is a deterrent to learning their life lesson. What the baby may need is support, such as comforting attention to what Source or God's remedies are, like homeopathic remedies, essential oils, and even nature. These remedies support the baby's journey instead of suppressing it. Have patience to identify the nature of the problem or issue; the Soul has nicely planned this situation out for you to assist in this learning experience and for you to move through it more joyfully and quickly.

It's funny when doctors tell you to take or give a medicine until the medicine is gone even after you feel better. Sometimes the medicine did nothing at all besides make you think you were doing something to help the situation. But the truth is, you may have felt better after ten days of completing a medication if you took the medicine or not. Many doctors do exactly what they are instructed to do by their peers, teachers, or medical groups. How many of them do you think take the time to connect to Divine guidance for answers? Why or why not? Not enlightened and in a hurry probably. Not patient. There is truth in the quote, "patience is a virtue."

Patience and stillness will provide the Divine wisdom to move gracefully through life's events. Patience has no time.

Patience stops the circumstance, to breathe and display needed information. Patience is all that is needed in true healing.

Patience brings you back to your Divine self, which is all knowing, all capable, all joy, and all love. This is you! Not a bad way to live, right?

Let Patience and Divine wisdom guide and light your path. Trust in the Divine! You are worth it! You are love!

CHAPTER 24

Everything Isn't as It Seems

Everything isn't as it seems. This book, for instance. It is written to inform you, to help you, but think about it: All that I have shared, you already know! Your Soul and your Spirit already know everything I've shared. *Why don't I consciously know this?* you might wonder. It goes back to the life lessons that need to be learned. If you know all that you knew when you were in Heaven, or Spirit form, the lessons wouldn't be as great. That's why we transform into a body. To learn lessons, to expand, and to evolve.

The ocean looks blue, but is it blue? Or is it just a reflection of the blue sky? An illness you have may seem real, but is it? Or is it an obstacle to direct you away from your Divine path? Once back on your path, it disappears as you perceive it. But, was it even there to begin with?

The mountains, are they real, or just an illusion made by your mind? We all are so different. We perceive and imagine things differently. It's magical how creative we are and how what we desire is perceived by others differently. We feel everything here in Heaven. Feelings and emotions are greater than sight.

Once again, we are all unique Spirits and beings.

My mom was losing things for while, like we all do on Earth. "Where are my keys?" she'd ask. When she went back to where she thought they might have been, she still could not find them. It was frustrating for her. Later she would revisit the place where she thought they were, and she would find them! How can that be? Everything isn't as it seems. There is a reason she was unable to find them initially and a reason she found them when she did. She may never know the reason, and it can be very frustrating for her. But it was necessary for her to see something, do something, move somewhere, or think something, when she could not find the lost item. Her Soul, Spirit, and Divine guides orchestrated the event for her growth, and it was exclusively for her. What might seem an annoyance can be an important lesson needed for you to expand and grow.

Your loved ones in Heaven can see your lessons you desired to learn while in your body and they continually assist and guide when able to. Sometimes we can only give support to not interfere with a life lesson. Behind everything that occurs in your life, there is a lesson to be learned. Look beyond the surface of an incident to obtain greater awareness and knowledge. Your greatest teachers are the situations you endure. No matter how big or small. It is never just an accident. It is always so much more.

CHAPTER 25

You Are Light

Divine light is what you are. Light is all there is. Dim light! Bright light! You get to choose how bright your light will be. A bright light is following Divine guidance correctly. A dim light is not. It's your choice. Deciding to shine brightly and follow your Divine path brings joy and pleasure. Deciding not to follow your Divine guidance dims your light and brings more hardships and struggles.

You know if you are a dim or bright light by how you feel. If you are happy and content, you are shining bright. If you are sad and depressed, you are not shining bright. Life situations and learning experiences are going to occur. This is what you arranged and signed up for before you were born. But it is all about how you process and perceive each event. Following a loved one's passing, did you allow yourself to grieve by feeling the emotions and then letting them go? Did you know that you were loved and guided through all that you did following the loved one's passing? Did you know that you are deserving of living an enjoyable life knowing that all was Divinely planned and orchestrated just for your growth and the growth of others involved? Did you know that when you were living in the past with the "would've," "could've," "should've" that this blocked you from moving forward? Did you know that living in the future kept and keeps you stuck, as well with the hoping and wishing for something that did and does not exist? Did you know that your loved ones in Heaven were pushing you to live in the present, to live in your light, because when you share and shine your light, you find the peace that you desire? This is the you that you were searching for, which is your Divine light that was always there but you chose to dim your light. It is a choice.

It is a choice to follow Divine direction or not to follow.

However, not to follow Divine guidance will result in feeling lost. In my Spirit form, I am my pure bright light. It is difficult to not shine bright in Heaven, as the lower vibration feelings of sadness and guilt do not resonate with us here. We see the big picture to all things. We see our life lessons, your life lessons, obstacles to living your Divine path, your energy, and your light. Our vibration in Heaven is love and love only. The lower vibrations fall away. We shine brightly to guide our loved ones into their bright light. Nothing else matters because it's an illusion that is made up to cause your light to go dim. Knowledge is everything. Enlightenment sets you free so you can live from your bright light and see all with love and compassion and move easily through all life's situations.

Life situations were created by you and for you to learn life lessons. We have discussed this already in previous chapters, but it is important to know that you have options. Knowing that you have choices is empowering; it awakens your dormant awareness. It releases that which does not serve you in your mission; it sets you free, free to be that free Spirit shining bright, and radiating love where ever you go. This is truly you! Choose to be you! Your Divine guides assist you in doing just that. Your guides can be Angels, your ancestors in Heaven, and other divine beings that care about you. You are loved greatly here. So greatly, it will rock your socks off. But you must ask, request, or demand our help so that we can assist you on your mission.

We want most of all for you to live free, live in abundance, live in your joy, with your passions, live helping others, live your life only for you, and to live in the light with the guiding light. Live your life choosing to shine bright for you and for all who are blessed to experience you!

We love you!

CHAPTER 26

This Is You!

Have you ever wondered what you are and who you are? Or even what you are here for? These are all good questions, and I have good answers for you. You are light. Your Spirit is light. When we leave our bodies, we are only our Spirits, which is light. What is the light? It is a spark, an extension of Source, but in the end it is Source energy. Source is what gave you existence in your body. Source breathes light throughout your veins. Source is your every existence. Source is *you*. Yes, I am saying Source or God is you. You are Source energy. You know all those cool things that God can do? Like heal, help, guide, support and love? Well you can do all that too! This Source or God light grows in all of us, and our lights grow together.

Our light is unique and special. We are all connected as one, as one Source light. We are all Source light energy moving in our Earth bodies, moving in our Spirit bodies, and evolving all the time.

On Earth, our light can dim when we forget who we are (God). When we forget, we can do all things like God. When we forget, we are all knowing like God. Why do we forget? It's because we listen to others and not to ourselves. We take on others' beliefs and we do not uphold what we know deep inside to be true. We get lost, and our light grows dim. But, your light still exists, always. You would not exist if your light did not exist. When we start remembering who we are (God), then our light begins to grow. When we remember who we are, we remember that we can do all things as God and our light grows bigger. When we return to knowing all things as God, our light shines brightly. This is who you are.

What are you put on Earth to do? To shine your light. To live peaceful in joy. To see, hear, know, and witness God and all his Divine helpers. To be guided and to help your fellow Earth beings to do the same. How? When you return to knowing who you are, your light radiates out to others. This ignites, inspires, and assists others to allow their own light to expand and return to its fullest capacity. Simple, right? It's actually very simple, but our well-ingrained falsehoods can get in the way. When you have felt a certain way for so many years, it is a well-ingrained habit. But guess what? Most of you have known who you are for several lifetimes, and that knowledge is stronger than your false beliefs. One only needs to allow this knowledge to resurface.

Then, with your intention, all this knowing begins to flood in. Your Divine assistance will deliver this knowledge to you in a timely manner so that your Earth body and mind can easily adjust.

What can you do now, to know you, which will expand your light? Know that you are God. Repeat powerfully, "I am God." This is influential, and it begins the process of letting the old beliefs disappear. An example of an old belief might be, "I can never do that." Instead say, "I am God. I can do all things," and truly feel the truth in this statement. Feel it in every fiber of your being and envision it expanding inside yourself. This simple exercise lets you remember you by confronting your old beliefs. By feeling yourself (God), this allows yourself to expand, to move into your bright shining light, and to live in your peace and joy. It's radiating your love and light out to others. It's assisting them to remember who they are, to evolve, to live in peace, and then guiding others to do so too. So cool, right? This is your Earth job. For those who choose this, as this is all a choice, will be rewarded greatly.

All Divine Heavenly beings are cheering you on and assisting you when you request their help. Remember, assisting is what we love to do, but you must ask us. I know you are probably wondering what this light energy is, aside from it being Source or God. It is love. All pure love. You are safe and protected in your endeavors since you are surrounded in a sea of love. How cool is that? See your love. Confront your beliefs that are not love by shining your God light and discarding those false beliefs. Radiate your love by sharing your love and watch as others begin to do the same.

Your Earth job is important, so lose the fear, which is only a false belief, and get moving. You can thank me later for the gentle kick in the butt to expand. Enlightenment is expansion!

CHAPTER 27

I Can See Clearly Now

"I can see clearly now; the rain is gone." The clouds have lifted. I see all the obstacles in my way. What does that mean? When you see the truth in everything by acknowledging the obstacles, all the obstacles fade away. The truth is you. The truth is us (Heavenly Spirits). The truth is in all of us. Everything else is an illusion for your benefit to learn, grow, and evolve.

Your possessions, job, health, and everything that you see with your vision is an illusion. It was all placed in front of you to teach you what you chose to learn in your lifetime, but it is not real. The only real thing is you, a being of light, love, and Source or God, whatever you choose to call your creator.

Think for a moment about being in your light body with no ailments, no house, no job, and no possessions. These are all "Earth things." Your light body is free and expansive, with nothing weighing it down. But you chose to have a "life on Earth" experience and you also chose to have the illusion. I was on Earth to enlighten and show others that they were so much more than their physical bodies. Your physical body is a very small part of you. Your physical body is not capable of all that you can do as a Light Being since your Light Being is unlimited and expansive.

When you walk on the beach, your Light Being is expanding. When you walk through nature, your Light Being is in love. It's no wonder I loved the beach and outdoors while I was in my body. Your Light Being expresses itself through your body because most Earth people cannot see a Light Being but they can see a body. Your Light Being is desiring to expand and feel love in your body. Have you ever met a person who was happy, free, joyful, and laughed a lot? Like me on Earth? This person is allowing their Light Being Spirit to grow in their Earth body. In contrast, have you ever met a person filled with anger and resentment and was not fun to be around? This person is not allowing their Light Being Spirit to expand. They have stopped the flow of love from the Divine Source. The Light Being is always present in a live body, but it can grow dim as previously discussed. A person like this is experiencing life lessons they chose to experience. They are learning and growing through their experiences. It is sad to see this in others; however, one must respect another's journey as they know what's best for themselves in all situations.

You have choices in life and you can choose to learn a life lesson through pain or you can choose to learn and move through experiences with ease. People who follow the less painful way allow their light and Divine guidance to shine through and show them the way. You are beautiful beings no matter what you choose. The choice to allow and follow Divine guidance will bring clarity to obstacles that arise and the knowledge to maneuver through these experiences gracefully with ease. With this enlightenment, we hope that it will be an easier choice to the best path for you on your amazing journey. Seeing clearly will take you far and wide in this lifetime. Doing so will bring you more joy and peace. It's your choice. Either way, you are always loved and you are always love!

CHAPTER 28

Can Life Get Any Better?

Can life get any better? Yes it can! You are going through life, you are feeling the joy and peace in everything. Life is good. Can it get better? Yes! Yes, it can! You want it to. Life, which is energy, keeps moving, and your Spirit wants it to keep moving forward in bliss with ease. But all good things must come to an end, even joy. For example, let's say a dream job you have is no longer fulfilling to you, an ideal relationship is no longer joyful, or a loved one who brought you joy transitions.

This merely means that it is now time to be open to a new joy, a new experience, a new adventure, a new path to take. Spirit pushes you to experience all that you are on Earth to experience. Spirit guides you and gives instructions for the next step to take. Spirit loves you so much that sometimes when you are too comfortable in one spot, it creates situations to nudge you forward. Illnesses occur, Earth death of loved ones may happen. Whatever it takes, your Spirit will lovingly push and guide you through to a new and more expansive joy and peace.

You came to Earth to live and evolve. When you reach a peaceful spot, you can't stay there because it's not evolving, and that is not living. That is stagnation. One must keep moving through whatever develops. Everything that is presented to you is an opportunity for growth, growth to evolve to a more enriched you, a more peaceful you, a more joyous you, and as Earth people say, a more Heavenly you. One must keep experiencing movement and growth to evolve into that Heavenly you.

Keep moving forward with your Spirit guiding you through ailments, for these will all vanish when you release your resistance to grow. Like a flower being guided by the sun to grow, you too are being guided to grow, live, and experience everything that comes to you. Allow your Earth self to step out of your way of your Divine light. Accept the love and respect all that has come your way for everything is there to assist you on your journey. Once you become aware of your resistance, you are enlightened to make a choice. A choice to think, do, and be in a different manner. Your Spirit prefers when you follow its guidance, but Spirit loves you and supports you no matter which path you choose to take.

Those who chose to release all resistance will move gracefully through the life lessons they chose for themselves in this lifetime. They continue to move forward, following the light and expanding their love, living in the present moment with joy, and knowing that all things must change to evolve.

Therefore, so must we.

We love you!
Enjoy your life!

Jeremy's Guide to Thrive During the Holidays When Your Loved One Has Transitioned

1. Know that your loved one never left you and never will. Even though we are not in body, we are always encouraging, guiding, supporting, and loving you all. When you accept this Truth, you will hear, see, and feel us. Get ready.

2. Know that we accomplished all we were supposed to accomplish in our Earthly Lives and we want you all to do the same. We want so much for you to release any grief and enjoy life. We are fine.

We are great. We are showering you with our love.

3. Live in the present moment. That's all that is real. Living in the past can make you sad. Living in the future can cause you stress. What is happening right now? Feel it! Smell it! Taste it! Hear it! Be grateful for the moment. Laugh, smile, play, and have fun! Enjoy company. Be grateful for coworkers and family. Love yourself and everyone around you. Even those who may seem difficult to love at times. Those are the ones who need your love. They will surprise you and bring you the most joy in life. I learned that in my Earthly Life.

4. Share good and funny memories about us with loved ones (you know I had a lot) and know that we love to hear you laugh. Have fun! Laugh lots! Earth Life is too short not to. Trust me on that one.

5. Know all is well. Have fun with loved ones and know we are always with you. Most importantly, live your life. Move above sadness and live life. Do whatever brings you joy and do it all the time. Stop doing what brings you down. You all deserve to live happy. Live it big and know we are all cheering for you. Feel our hugs when you hug others. We love hugs, so hug a lot!

Afterword

By Jeremy Logue

Thank you for reading my book. As my mom was putting the book together she said, "Jeremy, you keep repeating some things." This is because I want you guys to understand that you can live a happy life after your loved ones' transitions. In fact, you can live a happy life anytime you choose. We can help guide and assist you through life. We can teach you how things are from the perspective of a Spirit living in Heaven, like me, and that we are always with you. My book is titled, *Jeremy Shares His Love From Above,* but in truth I am right there by your side every time you think of me just like other Heavenly Spirits are with their loved ones as well.

I have enjoyed watching my mom. She has transformed from grieving for me to an understanding and truth about finding the peace she was searching for. She knows that I am always with her and that I am always guiding her. As my mom says, I talk a lot, but she loves it. It helps her to not miss me so much when she hears me all the time.

I hope that my book was enlightening and helpful to you as you venture onward in your amazing Earth Life journeys and beyond!

Love,
Jeremy

P.S. If you notice, I have two Chapter 10s in my book. Write your own book and you can do whatever you want. Ha! But let me explain. Ten breaks down to 1+0=1 and this is the one and only book that you need to live joyously and peacefully on Earth. Until I write my second book. My mom said, "What?" when I told her that. She doesn't care for writing, but she loves to listen to me. Also, I ended my book on Chapter 28. This is because 2+8=10 and 10 breaks down to 1 as I showed you, and you know what that means! You are catching on. My book size is 5x7 inches and 5+7= ? And what is my favorite number? Okay, no more for now, but I will catch you in my next book!

Afterword

By Rhonda Crockett Logue
(Jeremy's Earth Mother and Spirit Translator)

I too hope you enjoyed Jeremy's book. His writing and guidance helped me immensely to rise above my grief to be able to live a blissful and peaceful life.

I'd be lying if I said I do not miss Jeremy in body, but my understanding and acquired awareness assists me in living on Jeremy's Heavenly level in which I know he is always with me.

I am so proud of my boy and the life he lived on Earth. His heart. His compassion. The lives he touched and continues to touch. His love for us all is overflowing.

I love you, Jeremy, to the moon and back! I am so grateful for our Earth time together and our eternal Spirit time forever. You are truly amazing and full of light; you are a wonderful Spirit. Keep shining bright, my dear boy!

With Love and Angel Blessings,
Rhonda Crockett Logue

Jeremy with his Earth mother, Rhonda.

Afterword

By Antoniette Ibusag
(Jeremy's Earth Girlfriend)

I was lucky to have met the love of my life at a young age and to have seen him grow right before my eyes into the wonderful man that he became.

Jeremy, you made me so proud. Thank you for the adventures and the new ones we'll go on together (you in Spirit, of course). I am the person that I am today because of you. It gives me comfort knowing you are holding my hand throughout the rest of my whole life and that I am not facing this alone. I love you very much, Jeremy! Nothing will ever change that. You have my heart as it always been. I am excited to be working with Jeremy on our second book together, *The Greatest Love Story Ever Told.* It is a novel written to inspire young women to value themselves and to request nothing less than to be respected in their relationships with young men.

Forever and Always!
Antoniette Ibusag

Jeremy and Antoniette being wacky and crazy…as usual.

Live life! Be silly! Have fun!